my friend is struggling with . . .

Div...
of
Parents

Josh McDowell
& Ed Stewart

WORD PUBLISHING

NASHVILLE

A Thomas Nelson Company

Scripture quotations used in this book are from the Holy Bible, New International Version. Copyright © 1973, 1978, 1984, International Bible Society. Used by permission of Zondervan Bible Publishers.

Library of Congress Cataloging-in-Publication Data

McDowell, Josh.
    My friend is struggling with—divorce of parents / by Josh McDowell and Ed Stewart.
    p. cm. — (Project 911 collection)
    Summary: Describes what it is like when your parents divorce and suggests ways to deal with this situation from a Christian perspective.
    ISBN 0-8499-3794-9
    1. Children of divorced parents—Psychology—Juvenile literature. 2. Divorce—Religious aspects—Christianity— Juvenile literature. 3. Divorced parents—Juvenile literature. [1. Divorce—Religious aspects—Christianity. 2. Christian life.] I. Stewart, Ed. II. Title. III. Series
    HQ777.5 .M384 2000
    306.89—dc21

                                                                00-023365
                                                                CIP

Printed in the United States of America

00 01 02 03 04 05 QDT 9 8 7 6 5 4 3 2 1

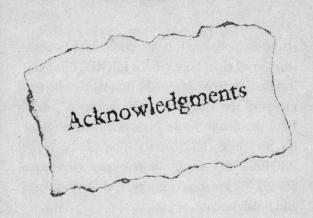

Acknowledgments

We would like to thank the following people:

David Ferguson, director of Intimate Life Ministries of Austin, Texas, has made a tremendous contribution to this collection. David's influence, along with the principles of the Intimate Life message, is felt throughout each book in this collection. David has modeled before us how to be God's comfort, support, and encouragement to others. We encourage you to take advantage of the seminars and resources that Intimate Life Ministries offers. (See pages 51–55 for more information about how this ministry can serve you.)

Dave Bellis, my (Josh) associate of twenty-three years, who labored with us to mold and shape each book in this collection. Each fictional story in all eight books in the PROJECT 911 collection was derived from the dramatic audio segments of the "Youth in Crisis Resource," which Dave personally wrote. He was also responsible for the design and coordination of the entire PROJECT 911 family of resources (see pages 56–59). We are so very grateful for Dave's talents and involvement.

Joey Paul of Word Publishing not only believed in this entire project, but also consistently championed it throughout Word.

JOSH MCDOWELL
ED STEWART

Jessica's Story

Fifteen-year-old Jessica Ingram knew what this evening's "family meeting" was about, even though Mom would not tell her anything specific. Jessica's sister, Karen, and brother, Mark, knew too. You'd have to be blind, deaf, and brainless not to understand what was going on. Dad and Mom were planning to announce to their three children that their "trial separation" had not worked and that they were getting a divorce.

The "Divorce Meeting" would be as horrible as the "Separation Meeting" had been three months earlier, Jessica knew. She would rather dive into a vat of sulfuric acid and disappear forever than be here tonight. Not literally, of course. She knew suicide was really a coward's way out of anything, besides being a sin. But what was the point of an Ingram family meeting when everyone would go away feeling even worse than they felt now? Why glorify a divorce by sitting down at the dinner table to announce it?

Flopped across her bed, Jessica turned up the volume on her CD headphones so she could not hear the silence in the house. Her eighteen-year-old sister, Karen, would be home from work in half an hour, just before the dreaded dinner meeting. If she were home now, Karen would be storming around the house slamming doors and cupboards and biting everybody's head off. *Venting,* she called it. Karen had always been very upfront with her anger about Mom and Dad's breakup, beginning in the middle of the "Separation Meeting" back in April. At least when Karen was venting, Jessica felt a little better. The silence was awful.

Their little brother Mark, twelve, was at home, but he was the exact opposite of Karen. After the "Separation Meeting," Mom had asked him how he was doing. He had just shrugged and had gone back to his computer games, acting as if nothing had happened. He was likely in his room right now with his own headphones on, systematically annihilating the evil warriors of Planet Zarg on his computer. Jessica knew that the family crisis was affecting him, that the kid was just blocking out his feelings or something. She was afraid of what might happen when it all caught up with him.

Mom was home too, Jessica knew, but she was buried in a corner of the house with one of her romance novels. Jessica thought she would feel better if her mother were in here ragging on her to clean up her room or do her chores. But Mom was apparently in retreat mode like she and Mark.

Dad was *not* home, of course. After the "Separation Meeting," he had moved into an apartment four miles away. Dad was bringing a couple of pizzas for dinner tonight, Mom had said. Jessica wrinkled her nose at the thought. What a cruel joke—to sit down and casually eat pizza while dismantling the family. Jessica wasn't hungry. She hadn't been hungry for three months. She hadn't slept well either, bothered by an itchy skin rash and horrible nightmares. It had all started in April. If this is how she felt after the separation, how much worse would she feel when Mom and Dad finally divorced? She didn't want to know.

As the music pounded in her ears, Jessica tried to pray. She had been a Christian almost a year now, having trusted Christ the previous summer at church youth camp. She had noticed a positive difference in her life since meeting Jesus. Prayer, Bible study, and worship were now significant parts of her life. But so far that difference had not extended to her family—particularly her parents. They only attended church about once every two months, when the youth music team, with Jessica singing, was on the program. And her parents had drifted farther apart in the past year, even though Jessica prayed for them regularly.

Praying for her parents' reconciliation now seemed almost hopeless. For one thing, Jessica assumed that the breakup was partly her fault. She could have been more obedient, compliant, and helpful, especially before becoming a

4

Christian. Her stubborn behavior at times had made Mom and Dad's life together more difficult, she knew. Jessica had asked God many times to forgive her for not being a better kid. With Dad's arrival less than an hour away, Jessica mainly prayed for Mark and Karen—and herself.

The "Divorce Meeting" was a sham of family life. Dad and Mark shoveled down pizza and talked about baseball as though it were a party. Jessica, Karen, and Mom took courtesy bites, then pushed their plates away and sat in silence. Mom seemed on the verge of tears. Karen had fire in her eyes, like a ticking time bomb set to explode. Jessica just wanted it to be over so she could go back to her room.

"Your mother and I have something to tell you," Dad announced finally. "Our problems have gotten worse instead of better since I moved out. The separation and counseling haven't helped. So we have decided to get a divorce. We want you kids to know that this is not about you; it's about Mom and me. We both love all three of you, and we will—"

Karen jumped to her feet so quickly that her

chair toppled backward and hit the hardwood floor with a crash. "This is so sick!" she screamed at both parents. "If you really loved us, you wouldn't do this to us. Why can't you work things out? I don't think you're really trying. I don't think you *want* to try." Spicing her anger with some strong words Jessica had never heard her sister use before, Karen vented big-time. Dad tried to interrupt a couple of times, but it was like spitting into the wind. So he just sat there and took it. Jessica knew it wouldn't change his mind. Mom squeezed her eyes closed and cried silently. Mark occupied himself by nibbling on pizza crust.

The more Karen blazed, the more Jessica could feel her own anger and hurt. Karen said things she wished she could say. It was as if her older sister were venting for both of them. And when Karen started crying, Jessica felt a swell in her throat and a warm tear on her cheek. Even though she could not agree with everything Karen said or how she said it, Jessica envied her sister's ability to blow off steam.

In less than two minutes—which seemed

more like two hours to Jessica—it was all over. Dad had said his piece, and Karen had exploded. Then Dad explained that he and Mom were still discussing living arrangements—who would live with whom and for how long. This was a new fly in the soup for Jessica. Dad had moved out and left the kids with Mom. Karen had told Jessica that she was pretty sure Dad was already dating and that he probably wouldn't want the girls or Mark living with him, for obvious reasons. Now Dad was talking about splitting up the Ingram family even more. And he was looking at Jessica when he said, "Maybe when school starts in September, someone would like to come live with me."

Jessica wasn't about to choose between her parents, but neither was she ready to become a Ping-Pong ball bouncing between them. Her room and her stuff were here. Jessica felt her place was with her mother, Karen, and Mark. She didn't know how she would tell her dad that she wanted to stay with Mom.

Jessica's father had a business appointment at 7:30, so he left a few minutes after 7:00. Jessica loved her dad, but she was glad to see him go. She had had enough of "family unity" for one night. Karen helped Mom clean up after dinner, Mark beamed back to Planet Zarg on his computer, and Jessica slipped away to her room and headphones.

She knew Mom and Karen would rehash all the gory details of the evening, which was the last thing Jessica wanted to do. A divorce was something that should be decided in private and then buried there, she assessed. It's not something you chat about, like how you liked a movie. And it's not something you talk about with friends, like, "I just got a new pair of Nikes on sale, and my parents are getting a divorce."

Jessica was suddenly aware of one benefit of being a Christian she had not previously realized. Her best friends were church friends, including the adult leaders, Doug and Jenny Shaw. And since none of her friends knew her family, they would not hear about the divorce unless she told them—which she would not. Even her best friend, Natalie Simmons, who had invited her to church camp a year ago and prayed with Jessica when she trusted Christ, knew only that her parents were separated. It would be important that Natalie help her keep the divorce a secret. But, of course, Natalie had to know about the divorce if she was going to help keep it a secret. So Jessica decided to tell her—and only her.

"Going to Natalie's, back by ten," Jessica called out to her mother on the way out the door. She was on her bike and headed down the driveway before her mother could respond. It felt good to be outside on a warm summer evening. It felt even better to be away from the house where the aroma of pizza kept reminding her of Dad's announcement. She wondered if she would ever be able to eat pizza again.

"Your parents are getting divorced? Oh, Jessie, I'm so sorry." Natalie's words took Jessica by surprise. There was so much feeling in them, so much love, and not an ounce of blame. The two girls had biked over to the city park and were sitting in adjoining swings when Jessica told Natalie about the dinner meeting at her house.

"Thanks, but it's a secret, all right?" Jessica responded.

"A secret? What do you mean?"

"I mean I don't want anybody at church to know," Jessica said insistently. "And now that you know, I don't even want to talk about it anymore."

"But why, Jessie?" Natalie probed.

Jessica hesitated, wavering on how honest she should be. Having told Natalie everything so far, she decided to be up front with her, even though it was difficult. "Because . . . because . . . the Ingram family isn't normal, all right? My parents are not Christians, and I'm not proud of the fact that they are doing this. I'd rather people didn't know." Then Jessica pushed herself back and lifted her feet to swing. Natalie did the same, and the two girls glided silently side by side for several minutes.

When the swings were almost still again, Natalie said, "What about Jenny?"

Jenny Shaw and her husband, Doug, in their thirties, were volunteer youth leaders at church. Jenny had also been present when Jessica trusted Christ last summer. Jenny had discipled Jessica one on one for several weeks after camp.

"What *about* Jenny?" Jessica said.

"She's a spiritual big sister to you," Natalie returned, "you said so yourself. I think you should tell Jenny what's going on at home. She could probably help you deal with your parents' divorce."

"I *am* dealing with it, Natalie. I'm just dealing with it . . . well . . . more privately than other people do."

"A divorce is a very big thing to handle privately," Natalie said, sounding a bit like a big sister herself.

"I told *you*, didn't I?"

"Yes, and I'm going to be praying for you," Natalie assured her. "I'm your friend, and I'm here for you. But I think Jenny may be able to help you deal with your emotions better than I can."

"Emotions? I'm not the emotional one in the family. That happens to be my sister, Karen." Jessica didn't want to argue with Natalie. But she didn't like her friend telling her what she needed, even if Natalie was right.

Natalie was silent for a minute, causing Jessica to wonder if she had given up. Then she said, "Remember when my older brother was killed two years ago?"

Jessica thought about it. "I barely knew you then. It was an accident at work, right?"

Natalie nodded. "Skip's death rocked the whole family pretty hard. I thought the best way to handle it was to get back to normal as soon as possible. So I told myself to get over it and get on with life. I didn't realize that there is a natural grieving process I had to go through. Jenny and Doug helped me get my feelings out where I could deal with them."

Jessica waited for the punch line, but Natalie said nothing more. She didn't have to. *A divorce is like a death,* Jessica recited to herself the unspoken admonition. *You need to grieve it; you need to pour your feelings out to someone who can help you deal with them. Jenny is your spiritual big sister. You need to go see her.*

After a few more minutes of silent swinging, Jessica said, "I'd better get home. I'm worried about Mark. I need to spend some time with him."

Before they got on their bikes, Natalie gave

Jessica a long hug. "I really hurt for you, Jessie. I'm so sorry you have to go through this."

Jessica returned the hug. "Thanks. Thanks for caring."

Jessica didn't take the most direct route home. She wanted to think a little more about whether she should tell Jenny Shaw about one of the saddest days in her life.

Time Out to Consider

Divorce is one of the saddest words in the English language, especially for the children of divorcing parents. And this sadness seems to affect a lot more people these days than in previous generations. In the middle of the twentieth century, the divorce rate in the United States was about 25 percent. In the 1960s that figure began to climb to a level approaching and sometimes exceeding 50 percent. It is likely that up to half the students in your school are from homes touched by the pain of parental separation or divorce. You may be reading these words right now because you are one of those students.

Divorce is sad and painful because it chips away at the very foundation of your early life. As a defenseless infant and young child, you looked to your parents as your primary source of love and security. That's how God designed the family to function. Even with the increased independence that comes with adolescence and young adulthood, you still derive a certain degree of security from a home where both parents are present and getting along. When that security base is disrupted because of separation or divorce, it will affect you in ways that may be difficult to understand and deal with, just as it has Jessica Ingram.

If your parents have recently separated or divorced, you may be experiencing a wide range of strong emotions. At different times you may feel angry, embarrassed, ashamed, guilty, bitter, afraid, confused, depressed, or alone. It may seem a little silly to say it, but how you feel is how you feel. You can't really do much to control your emotions. But you can better understand how you feel and deal with those feelings appropriately. One of the most helpful things you can do to get through this time in your life is to share your feelings and concerns with a trusted Christian friend. As Natalie suggested to Jessica, it will also be helpful to seek the comfort, support, and encouragement of a youth leader, minister, or other adult at your church.

How are you responding to the news that your parents are separating or getting a divorce? See if one or more of the following statements accurately represent your feelings.

I can't believe it, and I don't want to talk about it. It is perfectly natural to respond to your parents' breakup as if it isn't happening or by telling yourself that they won't go through with it. Jessica's brother, Mark, is trying to convince himself that there is no problem between his parents. Another form of denial is to idealize the absent parent or brag loudly and frequently about the breakup in order to cover your own anxiety. Or you may respond like Jessica, by refusing to talk about it. Denial is a normal way of coping with difficult situations, but in the long run, denial is not healthy.

I'm ashamed and embarrassed. Shame and

embarrassment are common responses to parents' separation or divorce. Like Jessica, you may be too embarrassed to tell some of your closest friends about what is happening in your family. You may feel that the breakup proves that there is something wrong with your family. You may be embarrassed by your parents' behavior toward one another. Abrupt changes in their lifestyle, such as one parent living away from you or dating, may bother you. You may also feel that your church or minister disapproves of you and your family. As tragic as divorce is, try to remember that it is *not* a reflection of your worth or your family's worth.

I feel guilty. I'm at fault. You may wonder, as Jessica does, if your behavior prompted your parents' decision to break up. You may feel responsible because of rebellion toward your parents, bad grades, a hot temper, fights with your siblings, or a failure to communicate your love to your parents. Perhaps your parents or other adults even told you that your attitude or behavior contributed to the divorce. These feelings may also prompt the inner urgency that you

16

must get your parents back together. But you are not responsible for breaking up the marriage or for putting it together again.

I feel angry and bitter. You may be angry about the breakup because it disrupts your family environment, creating disorder where before there was order. You may be angry or bitter because you resent being separated from one parent. Feelings of abandonment may spark your anger. You may resent being different from your friends whose families are still intact. You may have been the victim of one parent's resentment toward the other. The physical and financial burdens of the divorce may also be angering you. You may be angry about other aspects of the upheaval at home. In any case, you need to talk about your anger and get help dealing with it in healthy ways.

I'm worried and afraid. It is natural and common to react to your parents' problems with feelings of fear and anxiety. You may be worried about where you will live, where you will go to school, or where you will spend vacations. You may fear the reactions of your friends, other family members, and the church. You may be afraid that one parent and the grandparents and other relatives on that side of the family will abandon you. Jessica's unexpressed anger and fear have left her with no appetite, nightmares, and a skin rash. It is important to admit your fears and to talk honestly about them with your parents and with your youth leader or minister.

I feel relieved. In addition to other emotions, you may actually feel some relief that your mom and dad are separating or divorcing. This doesn't mean that you are heartless or without compassion for your parents. You may be thinking, *Anything is better than their constant fighting.* You may be hopeful that the separation will eliminate the abuse suffered by one parent, your siblings, or yourself. Just be sure that your relief isn't another form of denial or a subtle means of "getting back" at your parents. Since their divorce hurt you, you may be tempted to make them think you are glad they are splitting up.

I feel unloved, unworthy, and rejected. You may feel that the breakup of your parents' marriage means they don't love you. You may think,

Dad and Mom don't think I'm worth the effort of working out their problems. You may feel abandoned or rejected by the parent not living with you. You may feel that your friends, other family members, or people in your church look down on you. Or you may be struggling with other feelings of insecurity and rejection. Tell your parents and your youth leader or minister how you feel. Let them help you realize that the breakup is not a reflection of your worth, nor does it mean that your parents see you as unlovable.

I feel sad, confused, and depressed. The feelings you are experiencing now are similar to the grief someone feels when a friend or loved one dies. In the case of a divorce, parents may still be living, but the pain is no less real. You may experience times of sadness and confusion. You may feel lazy and listless, with little motivation to do anything. Your temper and emotions may be on edge, ready to erupt at the smallest irritation. Intense feelings may overcome you when you don't expect them. You may have difficulty expressing your feelings or realizing what sparked them. Grief is normal and healthy as long as it runs its course and does not spiral downward into desperation.

I feel helpless and hopeless. Your parents' separation or divorce may frustrate you because you can do little about it. You can't turn back the clock and undo whatever drove them apart. You can't change your parents' minds about the breakup. You can't mend their relationship. The reality and pain of the situation may leave you feeling helpless and hopeless. If you keep looking at the negative roadblocks, you will become more and more depressed. It is important to shift your attention away from what you *can't* do and focus on what you *can* do about dealing with your feelings.

I feel betrayed and alone. It is not unusual to experience a sense of alienation and loneliness as a result of parental divorce. You may feel that your parents have betrayed you. You may think, *No one understands what I'm going through; no one knows how I feel.* You may feel alienated from your church. You may feel suddenly distant from your friends, especially those whose parents are still together. You may even feel separated from

God. Such feelings may prompt you to withdraw physically from people, much as Jessica did. Or you may withdraw emotionally, as Jessica's brother, Mark, does with his video games. Despite the temptation to pull away from people at this time, you need to talk about your feelings with those who love you, such as your parents and youth leaders.

In the midst of all your feelings, you can have the confidence that God sees you and cares about you. The Bible says, "The LORD is close to the brokenhearted and saves those who are crushed in spirit" (Ps. 34:18), and "He heals the broken-hearted and binds up their wounds" (Ps. 147:3). God not only hurts when you hurt, but He also wants to comfort you, to hold you in His arms, to kiss your hurts, and to bandage your inner wounds. He invites you, through honest prayer and childlike trust, to "cast all your anxiety on him because he cares for you" (1 Pet. 5:7).

Your family situation may be disappointing, but it is not impossible. Simply talking to someone about your feelings and taking time to prayerfully work through the stages of grief will help you begin to cope with the changes in your family. Whenever you begin to feel desperate, don't suffer in silence and solitude. Tell someone who can help you, just as Jessica Ingram is about to do.

Jessica's Story

It took most of Friday morning for Jessica to work up the courage to call Jenny Shaw. She felt stupid about her hesitation because Jenny had been nothing but a kind, supportive friend and mentor in the faith ever since they'd met at camp the previous summer. Still, Jessica felt a little embarrassed to tell Jenny about her parents' divorce. But Natalie had encouraged her to do so, and she trusted her friend's judgment.

When she finally dialed Jenny's number—and fought off the urge to hang up before she answered, Jessica knew she had done the right thing. Without telling Jenny anything specific, Jessica asked if they could meet to "talk about something kind of important." Jenny said she could get away from the quick-print shop, which she and her husband, Doug, owned and operated, the following afternoon. It was supposed to be sunny and in the low 90s, so Jenny suggested they put on their swimsuits and lay out by the river. Jessica agreed, and Jenny promised to pick her up a little after 1:00.

That afternoon, Jessica waited to tell her story until they had spread a blanket on the grassy riverside knoll and slathered each other with sunblock. Sitting on the blanket and soaking in the sun, they were close enough to the river to see the children playing at the water's edge but far enough away from people to talk freely without being overheard.

Jessica didn't know how to start, so she just blurted out, "My parents are getting a divorce."

Jenny reacted in near shock. "Oh, Jessie, no," she said with a pained expression, placing a comforting hand on Jessica's arm. "I hadn't heard. I didn't know."

"Nobody knows, except Natalie," Jessica explained. "I didn't want anybody to know. But Natalie said I should talk to you."

"I'm so sorry, Jessie. This has to be very difficult for you."

Jessica could hear the comfort in Jenny's voice and feel her concern through her touch. She was already glad she had decided to share her news with Jenny. "It's been really . . . different . . . around our house," she conceded.

"Oh, Jessica, I really hurt for you," Jenny said. She seemed on the verge of tears, which brought a lump to Jessica's throat. "If you want to tell me about it, I'm here to listen."

Jessica didn't realize how ready she was to tell someone about her parents' conflict, separation, and impending divorce. For the next twenty minutes she poured out the story. There had been no screaming or fighting, she explained. The breakup might have been easier to accept if there had been. Her mom and dad had just silently drifted apart. They seemed to live in two separate worlds, even when they were home together. Dad had his demanding business schedule, golf, and service club activities. Mom lived in a fantasy world of romance novels, home and garden magazines, soap operas, and syrupy TV dramas. Her parents had so little in common, Jessica figured, that they would probably be happier living apart.

She held it together emotionally until she started talking about the living arrangements for the fall. "I think Dad wants either me or Karen to live with him," she said, starting to cry, "but I don't want our family split up even more. I love Dad, but I belong with Mom and Karen and Mark. I don't know what to do. I don't want this to happen."

Jessica didn't want to cry in public, even though there wasn't anyone near enough to pay attention. She tried to get a grip on her emotions. But when she felt Jenny's arm around her and saw the tears in her eyes, she couldn't hold back.

"It's okay, Jessie, go ahead and cry," Jenny said. "I know it hurts a lot. I'm so sorry. I'm here. Let it all out."

With Jenny's encouragement, Jessica let herself go and sobbed. It was the first time she had cried about her parents' breakup.

Wiping her eyes with a beach towel, Jessica began to feel some of the fire she had seen in Karen. The burst of tears had seemingly unlocked the gates to her emotions. "Why did Dad and Mom have to do this to us?" she demanded angrily. "It's not right. It's not fair, especially to Mark." The thought of her brother suffering in silence brought another brief surge of tears.

Jenny just held her and spoke reassuringly. "It hurts me that you have to go through this, Jessie, because I really care for you. But we can get through it together. I'm going to be here for you." Then she prayed the sweetest prayer that made Jessica feel that Jenny really was her older sister.

In a few minutes they were dabbing their eyes, blowing their noses, and even joking a little about how they must look to anyone glancing their way. Then Jenny was serious again. "A divorce is a lot like the death of a loved one. There are stages of grief that you go through when someone dies, and you may experience some of these stages as your parents' marriage dies. It might help you to know about them so you can deal with them when they happen."

"That's sort of what Natalie said," Jessica explained. "I guess it makes sense, but I don't know what the stages of grief are."

Jenny spent the next few minutes describing

the five stages of grief Jessica might encounter in the coming weeks. The simple explanation was enlightening, and Jessica recognized that she was already "grieving" her parents' divorce in certain ways.

Then Jenny said, "Would it be okay if we meet again—maybe a few times—to talk about how to process your feelings about the divorce and get through the stages of grief?"

"You mean, meet for breakfast and Bible study like we did last year after I trusted Christ?"

"Sure, if you're willing."

Jessica smiled. The time she had spent with Jenny after camp had greatly helped her solidify her commitment to follow Christ and had started her on a path of spiritual growth.

"Yes, I'd like that a lot," she said. Jessica and Jenny decided to meet the next two Saturday mornings for breakfast, with an option to add other Saturdays if needed. Then, leaving their towels on the blanket, they hurried down the knoll to cool off in the river.

For the first time since her parents' separation, Jessica did not feel alone in her pain and sadness. During the next week, she received encouraging phone calls and e-mails from Jenny. And Natalie called or dropped in occasionally just to say she was praying for her. It was difficult that first week, knowing that the divorce would soon be final. She also hurt for Karen and Mark, who were struggling in their own ways. But Jessica seemed better able to cope knowing that two very special people outside her family cared about her and were upholding her. And she hoped that the comfort and encouragement she had found in her mentor and friend would equip her to help her brother and sister.

Time Out to Consider

Like Jessica, you may recognize a number of emotions as a result of the separation or divorce of your parents. You may feel terribly sad, depressed, hopeless, abandoned, frightened, and even angry because of what happened. You may cry as you have never cried in your life. You may feel emotionally drained and exhausted. And you may get intensely angry at the situation, at one or both of your parents, or even at God for allowing it to happen. It is important to understand that these feelings are normal and natural. It is the way God wired you. Your emotions are a built-in release valve to help you handle the deep inner pain.

Jenny's simple advice to Jessica as they sat by the river was sound. She encouraged Jessica not to bottle up her feelings, but to let her grief flow out. Jenny sat there to hurt and cry with her. This response reflects Jesus' words in Matthew 5:4: "Blessed are those who mourn, for they will be comforted." Mourning is the process of getting the hurt out. You share how sad you feel so others can share your pain and hurt with you. This is God's design for blessing you and beginning to heal the pain that accompanies the divorce of your parents.

A divorce can be seen as the death of a marriage. You may react to your parents' divorce much as you would react to the death of a parent, sibling, or friend. Grief is a common process most people go through after such sad events. The grieving process, which may continue for several weeks or months, has five clearly identifiable stages. Some of these stages overlap with the responses discussed earlier. No two people go through the process in exactly the same way, and the stages often overlap and recur. But you will likely find yourself responding to your family tragedy something like Jessica did.

One of the first responses to grief is *denial*. You may find yourself at times unwilling to believe that such a terrible thing is happening to you. Jessica displayed this response when she retreated to her room and refused to talk about what was happening at home. One of the ways your mind and emotions will try to handle the shock of your grief is to say, "No way, this is not happening to me."

A second stage in responding to grief is *anger*. When grappling with the inevitable question "Why did this happen?" you may find yourself lashing out angrily because there is no reasonable answer to that question. You have lost a large measure of your personal security, and it seems terribly unfair. Like Jessica's sister, Karen, your anger may be vented at one or both of your parents for going through with the divorce. Or like Jessica, your anger may be at the divorce itself more than at the participants. Your anger may even be directed at yourself because you suspect that you were somehow to blame for what happened.

A third stage of grief is *bargaining* with God for relief from the awful event and its consequences. You may find yourself secretly trying to cut a deal with God, vowing to change your behavior if He will bring your parents back together. Jessica may be motivated to bargain with God by her sense of false guilt over not being a better child, which she fears has caused the breakup in some way. You may be prompted to try to cut a deal with God both to reunite your parents and to make up for perceived failures.

Another stage of grief is *depression*, which may come when you realize that the divorce is really going to happen. It's the feeling of overwhelming sadness or hopelessness over the loss. Depression may be accompanied by fear, anxiety, or insecurity about living without one of your parents being there. Loneliness is another facet of depression. Jessica was already experiencing the loneliness of living apart from her father.

The final stage of grief is *acceptance.* As time goes by and the other stages of grief diminish, you will be able to accept the reality of the divorce and begin to deal with it constructively. Even as this stage becomes dominant, you may still experience pangs of denial, anger, and depression. But they will be minimal compared to the more positive sense that God is working out your experience for good (see Rom. 8:28).

In some cases it takes many weeks to successfully navigate all five stages of grief. Some of the emotions and thoughts that you experience during this time may be new to you or stronger than ever before in your life. You may wonder if there is something wrong with you for reacting in these ways. There is not. You are going through a common response to the very sad event in your life.

The only real danger as you move through these stages is allowing yourself to express your feelings in inappropriate or unhealthy ways. For example, if Jessica's depression caused her to attempt suicide, she would be responding to her grief in an improper and unhealthy way. It is wise not to respond impulsively to any of the strong emotions you encounter as you move through the stages of grief.

In addition to the stages of grief, there are many more emotions and responses to sort through. Thankfully, Jessica Ingram has a "big sister" to help her.

Jessica's Story

As soon as they sat down at the pancake house for their first meeting, Jenny asked Jessica, "How did it go this week?"

Jessica shrugged. "All right, I guess. It's still hard to accept that my parents are getting a divorce. I'm glad you told me about the grieving process. I think I have been experiencing denial and a little depression this week."

"That's why I wanted us to get together a couple of times," Jenny said. "The best way to work through those experiences is to talk about them and focus on what is happening behind the feelings."

After they ordered breakfast, Jenny pulled a sheet of paper from her purse and passed it over to Jessica. "The other day I was thinking about how you might be feeling about the divorce," she began. "So I started writing down a number of different feelings that may apply. Are there any on this list you have experienced?"

Jessica read the first word aloud, "'Disbelief,'" and stopped. "I can sure identify with that one. I can't believe my parents are getting a divorce. I really don't *want* to believe it. One night last week I dreamed that Dad was back home again and everything was all right between him and Mom. It was so real that I got up in the morning almost expecting to find Dad at the kitchen table drinking coffee and reading the paper. But, of course, he wasn't there."

"Disbelief is a form of denial," Jenny informed her. "It's the brain's way of trying to maintain a level of stability in the face of great stress. Some people show their denial by refusing to talk about a problem or even to admit there is a problem. Some may admit there is a problem but deny that they are affected by it. Denial is a defense mechanism, but it usually isn't healthy. Eventually you must admit that the divorce is happening and that your life will be different because of it."

Jessica nodded slowly. "I understand. Living in a dream world isn't healthy, and it isn't right. You can't deal with a problem effectively if you deny it exists."

"That's an important insight, Jessie," Jenny said.

"I'm afraid Mark has slipped into denial big-time," Jessica added. "He won't talk about Mom and Dad. Whenever I bring up the subject, he retreats to his video games."

"Maybe God will use you to help him," Jenny said. "I have been praying for Mark and Karen just as I have been praying for you."

Jenny kept reading the list aloud. "'Shame,' 'embarrassment,' 'anger,' 'guilt'—hm, I guess I have been feeling a little guilty too."

"Tell me about it."

Jessica hesitated at the painful thought. The waitress arrived with glasses of juice, and Jessica was grateful for a few extra seconds to frame her answer. "I think Mom and Dad's problems are partly my fault. I haven't always been a model child at home. When I turned thirteen, I felt pretty independent. So one night I violated my curfew— on purpose—by about a half-hour. I got into a big argument with my parents about it when I got home. I remember Dad shouting, 'You make it very hard on your mother and me when you do things like this, Jessica. Marriage isn't easy, and your behavior doesn't make it any easier.' That's when I realized they weren't getting along very well and that I might be part of the problem."

"It saddens me to hear that you feel responsible for your parents' breakup," Jenny said compassionately, "and I can see how you might feel that way. But you are not to blame. You may not be a model child, but no child is. Parents have to deal with life's difficulties, including disagreements with their children. Your parents are responsible for their relationship."

"But Dad said—"

Jenny quickly interrupted. "Your dad may find it hard to accept full responsibility for his problems. A lot of people do. He probably didn't mean to hurt you by it, but pointing to your misbehavior allowed him to shift some of the blame away from himself."

Jessica pondered Jenny's words for a moment. "So it's not my fault after all?"

"No, the breakup is not your fault, and getting your parents back together is not your responsibility. They are adults. They are responsible for their relationship. All you can do is pray for them and love them."

Jessica sat back and released a long sigh. "That's kind of a relief."

"It should be," Jenny said. "You don't have to feel guilty anymore."

The waitress arrived with two orders of pancakes. As they ate, Jessica continued to read through Jenny's list and noted a few more feelings she had experienced. Jenny's insightful questions and comments helped her defuse some of the pain behind the feelings.

Jenny also asked how the rest of Jessica's life was going. Jessica sheepishly admitted that she felt so bummed out that she had ignored most of her chores around the house. She was hopelessly behind on the laundry and gardening, which were her responsibilities. Jenny surprised her by pulling out a cell phone and dialing Natalie right then. In less than two minutes Jenny had arranged for Natalie to come over later in the day to help Jessica catch up on her work at the house.

After getting past a flash of embarrassment, Jessica sensed a wave of relief. Usually very good about keeping up with her work, she had been feeling too down to stay busy. Knowing that Natalie was coming to help her seemed to lift that weight off her shoulders.

The time flew by quickly, and Jenny had to leave for work. But they agreed to meet again the next Saturday to continue their chat. Jessica left the pancake house that day grateful for Jenny's loving concern and practical help and very hopeful for the week ahead.

Time Out to Consider

In the process of mourning your painful situation, you have three significant needs that can be met by spiritual leaders like Jenny and Christian friends like Natalie. It is important to be aware of these needs and to allow others to meet them.

You need comfort. Your greatest need as you first become aware of your parents' separation or divorce is for others to comfort you. That's how Jenny responded when Jessica blurted out the news of her parents' divorce. In a time of pain and sorrow, our greatest comfort comes when others sorrow with us. One major way God shares His comfort with us is through other people. The apostle Paul wrote, "God . . . comforts us in all our troubles, so that we can comfort those in any trouble with the comfort we ourselves have received from God" (2 Cor. 1:3, 4).

What is comfort? Maybe it will help to see first what comfort is *not*. Comfort is not a "pep talk" urging you to hang in there, tough it out, or hold it together. Comfort is not an attempt to explain why bad things happen to people. Comfort is not a bunch of positive words about God being in control and everything being okay. All of these things may be good and useful in time, but they do not fill our primary need for comfort.

People comfort us primarily by feeling our hurt and sorrowing with us. Jesus illustrated the ministry of comfort when His friend Lazarus died (see John 11). When Jesus arrived at the home of Lazarus's sisters, Mary and Martha, He wept with them (see vv. 33–35). His response is especially interesting in light of what He did next: raise Lazarus from the dead (see vv. 38–44).

Why didn't Jesus simply tell the grieving Mary and Martha, "No need to cry, My friends, because in a few minutes Lazarus will be alive again"? Because at that moment they needed someone to identify with their hurt. Jesus met Mary's and Martha's need for comfort by sharing in their sorrow and tears. Later He performed the miracle that turned their sorrow to joy.

We receive comfort when we know we are not suffering alone. Paul instructed us, "Rejoice with those who rejoice; mourn with those who mourn" (Rom. 12:15). When you experience sorrow, people may try to comfort you by cheering you up, urging you to be strong, or trying to

40

explain away the tragic event. These people no doubt care about you and mean well by their words. But they may not know what comfort sounds like. Hopefully, there will also be someone around like Jenny Shaw who will provide the comfort you need. You will sense God's care and concern for you as this someone hurts with you, sorrows with you, and weeps with you. Jenny Shaw is a good example of what real comfort looks like in a sad and painful circumstance.

You need support. Jessica needs more than comfort to get through the pain of her parents' divorce. She also needs support. What's the difference between comfort and support? People supply the comfort you need when they share your sorrow emotionally. People supply the support you need by helping you during this time in practical, helpful ways. The day-to-day tasks of life go on even during difficult and painful circumstances. But you may have little attention or energy for such things because you are dealing with such a heavy emotional burden. You need temporary help just to get these things done. You need the help of people who are committed to obeying Galatians 6:2: "Carry each other's burdens, and in this way you will fulfill the law of Christ."

Jenny provided support for Jessica by offering to meet with her and help her work through her maze of confusing thoughts and feelings. Jenny offered practical, scriptural advice about how Jessica should respond to each emotion. And she even arranged for Natalie to come over and help with some mundane but necessary chores Jessica was just too bummed out to complete.

You may be tempted to ignore or to refuse the support offered by others. You may feel that you can handle it yourself, or you may not want others to be bothered with things you normally do for yourself. Resist that temptation. God put Galatians 6:2 in the Bible because He knows there are times we should rely on the support of others. This is such a time. Let other people do things for you and be grateful for their help. It is one of the ways God is providing for your needs at this time.

What if you have a need and nobody steps up to offer help? Ask for it. There is nothing wrong with telling a trusted friend, a youth leader, or your minister about your need and asking for help. For example, had Jenny not called Natalie and asked her to help, it would have been appropriate for Jessica to ask for her friend's help. In most cases, people are more than willing to help out; they just don't know what needs to be done. Feel free to help people support you at this time by letting them know what you need.

You need encouragement. In addition to comfort and support, you need the encouragement of others. You receive encouragement when someone does something thoughtful to lift your spirits. Jessica was encouraged whenever Jenny called or e-mailed her just to say she was praying for her. She was encouraged when Natalie came over to see how she was doing. Encouraging deeds like these may not seem as practical as someone helping out with chores, but they are just as necessary.

Once again, if you do not receive the encouragement you need, ask for it. It's okay to tell someone who cares about you, "I need a hug" or "I just need you to be with me for a while."

The comfort, support, and encouragement

of people who love you will make a significant difference in how you get through the pain of your parents' breakup. Jessica is about to explain the difference she has experienced since the "Divorce Meeting" almost a month earlier.

Jessica's Story

Doug Shaw said he was tired of having breakfast alone on Saturday mornings, and that's why he came with Jenny to the pancake house for the last of her three breakfast meetings with Jessica. The three of them laughed at the comment. Actually, Doug came at Jenny's invitation—with Jessica's approval. Doug had also been a source of comfort, support, and encouragement in the month since Jessica's father had announced the divorce.

"This was an especially hard week, wasn't it, Jessie?" Jenny said after Doug asked the blessing on the plates of pancakes in front of them.

Jessica nodded. "Mom and Dad's divorce was final yesterday. It was kind of a black Friday."

"So how are you doing, Jessie?" Doug asked.

Jessica felt pretty upbeat and tried to sound

that way. "Actually, I'm doing okay. I've been hoping and praying all month that my parents would change their minds and get back together. But it didn't happen." Then she added quickly with a smile, "Don't worry: I'm not in denial. I know that Dad and Mom have gone their separate ways. As much as I wish it hadn't happened, I no longer blame myself for it. I still pray that they will find Christ and get back together—in that order."

"That's a good way to pray," Doug assured her.

"But yesterday was still a sad day for you?" Jenny probed.

Jessica chewed and swallowed a forkful of Swedish pancake before answering. "Right. I happened to be outside when the postman came by. The official letter was in the stack of mail. I was there when Mom opened it."

"That must have been difficult for you," Jenny said.

Jessica thought for a moment. "Mom seemed relieved that it was all over. I think that bothered me as much as seeing the divorce finalized in black and white. It hurt a little that she was almost glad to be rid of Dad. I guess she doesn't realize that she divorced Dad, but I didn't. He's still my dad, and I love him."

Doug put his fork down. "I feel sad for you, Jessie, that your mom doesn't understand your feelings for your dad."

Jessica rubbed her chin with her thumb. "Thanks, but I'm doing a lot better about things like that. It's like Jenny says, time really helps heal the emotions. I'm able to deal with the hurt a lot better, thanks to our chats over the last three weeks." She flashed a smile of appreciation Jenny's way.

Jenny winked her acknowledgment. Then she said, "How are Karen and Mark doing?"

"Karen still slams a door or two sometimes," Jessica said, "but I think she's getting over it. And Mark seems to be opening up more. I go in and talk to him for a few minutes every night. When I ask how he's feeling, he usually doesn't have much to say. So this week I tried a different approach. I used that list you gave me. I asked him questions, like, 'Mark, do you feel embarrassed about Mom and Dad's divorce? Do you feel sad?' It's a little easier for him to answer yes or no. When he says yes, I try to comfort him and encourage him in that area, like you have done for me."

Jenny beamed. "That's wonderful, Jessie. It reminds me of Second Corinthians one, verses three and four. You are comforting Mark with the comfort you received." Then she turned to Doug. "I think Jessie is ready to meet Alyson. What do you think?" Doug smiled and nodded.

Jenny turned back to Jessica. "Alyson Gilbert is a new seventh grader in our middle-school group. We found out last week that her parents were divorced in the spring. She moved here with her mother. Doug and I were wondering if you would like to meet Alyson and share your experience with her."

Jessica felt both honored and scared at the same moment. "I don't know about that. I'm not really a counselor. I don't know my Bible that well yet."

"We're not asking you to counsel Alyson," Doug said. "Just share your comfort and encouragement with her as a friend, like you're already doing with Mark. Tell her your story and what you are learning about getting through your parents' divorce. Can you do that?"

Jessica glanced back and forth between Doug and Jenny. "Just do what I'm doing with Mark?" she said. "That's all?" The couple nodded in unison. Suddenly it sounded very simple. "Sure, I can do that," she said confidently. "When can I meet Alyson?"

Doug picked up his fork. "Not until I finish my apple pancakes," he said with a big laugh.

Time Out to Consider

As Jessica is discovering, one of your best allies for dealing with the separation or divorce of your parents is time. The old proverb, "Time heals all wounds," contains a nugget of truth. The Bible says it this way: "Weeping may remain for a night, but rejoicing comes in the morning" (Ps. 30:5). Accept the fact that it will take time for you to get over the tragedy in your family. You need time to process the jumble of feelings and thoughts. You need time to talk out your feelings with mature, compassionate Christian friends and leaders. As the weeks pass, your sorrow will diminish and your life will return to a fairly normal pattern. Give time a chance to work for you by not expecting the pain and confusion to go away too soon.

Jessica Ingram has been through a tough experience in the last month. Watching her parents finalize their divorce has been a painful emotional blow. But she is getting through it. She is able to separate reality from the fantasy of denial and false guilt. And she is even able to empathize and share comfort with her brother and others. Jessica has not finished the grieving process yet, but she is making great progress.

The pain of your parents' divorce may be so great right now that you wonder if you will ever get back to normal. Keep these keys in mind as you trust God to get you through this difficult experience.

Let your sorrow be expressed. God designed your emotions to help you vent your disappointment, anger, and sorrow. Don't stuff your feelings inside; let them out so your heart can start healing.

Allow others to comfort you, support you, and encourage you. God's design for healing your heart includes involving other people. Let loving family members and friends comfort you, encourage you, and care for you in practical ways.

Give yourself time to grieve. Moving through the stages of grief—denial, anger, bargaining, depression, and acceptance—may take weeks or months. Be assured that, as time passes, things will get better.

Allow God to use you to comfort, support, and encourage others. Your experience of receiving comfort from others has uniquely equipped you to help others in sorrow. It may take time, but you will have an opportunity to pass along comfort, support, and encouragement to someone else who is struggling with separation or divorce in his or her family.

Isn't it encouraging to know that God can help someone like Jessica through the difficult experience of her parents' divorce? Even better, He can do it for you too.

APPENDIX

MORE ABOUT INTIMATE
LIFE MINISTRIES

Several times in this book I have mentioned the work of Dr. David Ferguson. David's ministry has had such a profound effect on me in the past several years that I want you to have every opportunity to be exposed to his work and ministry. David and his wife, Teresa, direct a ministry called Intimate Life Ministries.

WHO AND WHAT IS INTIMATE LIFE MINISTRIES?

Intimate Life Ministries (ILM) is a training and resource ministry whose purpose is to *assist in the development of Great Commandment ministries worldwide.* Great Commandment ministries—ministries that help us love God and our neighbors—are ongoing ministries that deepen our intimacy with God and with others in marriage, family, and the church.

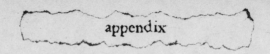

Intimate Life Ministries comprises:

- A network of **churches** seeking to fortify homes and communities with God's love;

- A network of **pastors and other ministry leaders** walking intimately with God and their families and seeking to live vulnerably before their people;

- A team of **accredited trainers** committed to helping churches establish ongoing Great Commandment ministries;

- A team of **professional associates** from ministry and other professional Christian backgrounds, assisting with research, training, and resource development;

- **Christian broadcasters, publishers, media, and other affiliates,** cooperating to see marriages and families reclaimed as divine relationships;

- **Headquarters staff** providing strategic planning, coordination, and support.

How Can Intimate Life Ministries Serve You?
ILM's Intimate Life Network of Churches is an effective, ongoing support and equipping relationship with churches and Christian leaders. There are at least four ways ILM can serve you:

1. *Ministering to Ministry Leaders*
ILM offers a unique two-day "Galatians 6:6" retreat to ministers and their spouses for personal renewal and for reestablishing and affirming ministry and family priorities. The conference accommodations and meals are provided as a gift to ministry leaders by cosponsoring partners. Thirty to forty such retreats are held throughout the U.S. and Europe each year.

2. *Partnering with Denominations and Other Ministries*
Numerous denominations and ministries have partnered with ILM by "commissioning" them to equip their ministry leaders through the Galatians 6:6 retreats along with strategic training and ongoing resources. This unique partnership enables a denomination to use the expertise of ILM trainers and resources to perpetuate a movement of Great

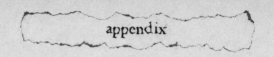
Commandment ministry at the local level. ILM also provides a crisis-support setting to which denominations may send ministers, couples, or families who are struggling in their relationships.

3. *Identifying, Training, and Equipping Lay Leaders*

ILM is committed to helping the church equip its lay leaders through:

- *Sermon Series* on several Great Commandment topics to help pastors communicate a vision for Great Commandment health as well as identify and cultivate a core lay leadership group.

- *Community Training Classes* that provide weekly or weekend training to church staff and lay leaders. Classes are delivered by Intimate Life trainers along with ILM video-assisted training, workbooks, and study courses.

- *One-Day Training Conferences* on implementing Great Commandment ministry in the local church through marriage, parenting, or singles ministry. Conducted by Intimate Life trainers, these conferences are a great way to jump-start Great Commandment ministry in a local church.

4. *Providing Advanced Training and Crisis Support*

ILM conducts advanced training for both ministry staff and lay leaders through the Leadership Institute, focusing on relational ministry (marriage, parenting, families, singles, men, women, blended families, and counseling). The Enrichment Center provides support to relationships in crisis through Intensive Retreats for couples, families, and singles.

For more information on how you, your church, or your denomination can take advantage of the many services and resources, such as the Great Commandment Ministry Training Resource offered by Intimate Life Ministries, write or call:

Intimate Life Ministries
P.O. Box 201808
Austin, TX 78720-1808
1-800-881-8008
www.ilmministries.com

Connecting Youth in Crisis

Obtain other vital topics from the PROJECT 911 Collection...

Experience the Connection

JOSH McDOWELL'S PROJECT 911

For Youth & Youth Groups

This eight-week youth group experience will teach your youth the true meaning of deepened friendships—being a 911 friend. Each lesson is built upon scriptural teachings that will both bond your group together and serve to draw others to Christ.

This optional video is an excellent supplement to your group's workbook experience.

As follow-up to your youth group experience, continue a young person's friendship journey by introducing them to a thirty-day topical devotional journal and a book on discovering God's will in their life.

Experience the Connection

For Adults & Groups

This watershed book is for parents, pastors, youth workers, or anyone interested in seeing youth not only survive but thrive in today's culture.

Book on Audio

This book, directed specifically to fathers, offers ten qualities to form deepened relationships between dads and their kids.

Begin your church-wide emphasis with an adult group experience using this five-part video series. Josh provides biblical insights for relationally connecting with your youth.

Experience the Connection

For Youth Workers

A one-on-one resource to help you provide a relational response and spiritual guidance to the 24 most troubling issues youth face today.

This handbook brings together over forty youth specialists to share their insights on what makes a successful youth ministry.

Contact your Christian supplier to obtain these PROJECT 911 resources and begin experiencing the connection God intended.

ABOUT THE AUTHORS

JOSH MCDOWELL, internationally known speaker, author and traveling representative of Campus Crusade for Christ, International, has authored or coauthored more than fifty books, including *Right from Wrong* and *Josh McDowell's Handbook on Counseling Youth*. Josh and his wife, Dottie, have four children and live in Dallas, Texas.

ED STEWART is the author or coauthor of numerous Christian books. A veteran writer, Ed Stewart began writing fiction for youth as a coauthor with Josh McDowell. He has since authored four suspense novels for adults. Ed and his wife, Carol, live in Hillsboro, Oregon. They have two grown children and four grandchildren.